GYPSY

Where Are You?

This is our true story. We did not change our names because each of us can testify to an afternoon that God answered prayers and asked each of us, "Where are you?"

DEDICATED to Jesus, our sweet Savior, who asked Adam and Eve, "Where are you?" He asks each of us that question today. Adam and Eve hid from God, covered in leaves behind a bush. Are you hiding behind your bush of disabilities, doubts or fear? Jesus is Light and Truth. Let Him help you find your way. He assures us that we are not lost if we remain in Him.

"I am the vine; you are the branches. If you remain in me and I in you,
you will bear much fruit; apart from me you can do nothing."

JOHN 15:5

What a sweet story of hope and truth! I read this beautifully written and illustrated book with my children who are dyslexic. They related to the character, Zach, as he greatly struggled in school. Through a series of difficult events, Zach learned that God answers his prayers because He cares for him. Life isn't easy (for kids or adults), but when we learn to place our hope in God, He makes a way. This story is a beautiful picture of that truth! Luke 19:10 — **Debby H., Schriever, LA - Home Schooling Mom and Lover of Children's books.**

I really enjoyed how the family treated Gypsy like a human and would not stop searching for her when she was lost. I found it very interesting that Zach was having trouble in school just like me. I also liked how they prayed to God when they were in trouble. I think the moral of the story is that you can trust God to help. They prayed for help in finding the lost things. Zach felt lost in school. His dad's bike was lost. Gypsy was lost. Zach learned that God could help him with school. This story really changed my point of view. It is an amazing story that teaches about God. — **Andrew, Schriever, LA (11 years old)**

Zach's message to Andrew:

I know school can be hard and learning can be difficult for you because you see things differently. I am glad my story helped you. I still get lost if I lose my focus. I, too, must remember to look for God's guidance.

I enjoyed this book because it shows how God works in our lives. Even when people think it is just a coincidence, we know it's God. —**Riley W. Reece (8 yrs old)**

Truly, this is an inspiring book to encourage us in our walk with the Lord; in faith; in the power of prayer; and in the reminder that God loves each of us! There is a beautiful, yet haunting question that we each need to answer daily … "Where Are You?" I fell in love with this family, their situation and Gypsy through the beautiful illustrations that brought the book to life! This is a heart wrenching story of faith, prayers, love and trusting God. Be assured of the fact: "God hears and answers prayers!" Isaiah 65:24 — **V Jeffers, Author of I'll Fly Away and Juan Prayer.**

I enjoyed reading this beautifully illustrated book and enjoyed it thoroughly! Having a degree in Fine Arts, I was truthfully as interested in seeing the illustrations as the text. When I was in grade three, I looked forward to reading a book ONLY if it were illustrated. When we went to the library as a class, I ALWAYS picked out a book to read based on the "pretty" pictures! I admired Jody Eklund's artistic contributions and believe they will appeal to many little kiddos who consider the book for its wonderful, true-life story. — **Cheryl Sinz, Author of Bird Legs.**

This is my favorite book because my Dad drew the pictures.
—**Kaylin (6 years old)**

Written by

Judy Ginter

&

Illustrated by

Jody Eklund

*Z*ach felt miserable. He hated school, especially today. He was trying to read, but the letters marched around the page in a scrambled mess.

Zach wanted to scream, "What is that word? Is it 'Dog' or 'God'?" Tears filled his eyes, "Is this a cruel joke? God, You made my eyes look like other kids, but they see everything backwards. Why didn't You make my eyes see things forward?"

Zach rubbed his eyes and buried his face in his arms to hide his tears from the other kids. He felt sorry for himself. "School is too hard for me. It isn't my fault that I have dyslexia and will never be like everyone else. God, You know I am not superman. My brain, eyes and fingers don't work the way I want them to. It's so hard to write the right letters to form words. I feel so lost and, I am too tired from trying. I want to quit." Zach sighed loudly. "I just want to forget about school and think about my puppy."

Zach's puppy was named Gypsy. She was a 3-month-old black Lab and already weighed 25 pounds. She was going to grow into her large paws and end up the size of a bear. She was shiny black all over, except for the whites of her eyes and her pink tongue. She used her pink tongue to give Zach wet-dog kisses.

Zach loved Gypsy and she loved him. She always greeted him with bounces and licking kisses. She sat next to him when he was glad and even when he was sad. She chased the balls he threw. She wiggled all over when he gave her a cookie-bone. She never got angry with him. She was loyal and loved him more than anyone. She thought everything he did was just right.

That day, as Gypsy explored her backyard, she sniffed the bushes and peeked through the fence slats, wishing a squirrel would venture down from the apple tree.

Before she found a squirrel to chase, a friendly man in a uniform opened the back gate. He walked into the yard.

"Hello," he said to Gypsy. He walked past her to the gas meter and wrote numbers in his book. Then, he walked back to the gate. He pulled it shut but it didn't close all the way.

Gypsy watched him until he left. She saw that the gate was open a crack. Gypsy bounced to the gate. She nudged it with her nose and peeked out. She saw glorious things. She decided to explore this marvelous world.

She ran from her yard, gleefully chasing butterflies and birds, and sniffing noses with friendly dogs. She explored her neighborhood, free from her leash for the first time.

But soon, she became confused. She didn't recognize anything and couldn't find her house. Gypsy looked for her house for a long time. Her paws became sore and tender. She could hardly walk. After licking her sore paws, she decided to rest them.

After searching and searching, she discovered a house that looked like her house. It had a fence and backyard like her house. She limped into the yard through the open gate.

However, this was not her yard. There was a huge trampoline in the backyard. Gypsy had never seen one before. She decided to check it out. She easily climbed the steps that led to the top. It was bouncy. Her legs acted silly as she walked across it. She playfully stumbled and jiggled. The black mat was

warmed by the sun. It felt as good as lying on Zach's waterbed. The sun on her back and the warmth of the black trampoline mat made her sleepy. After a big stretch and yawn, she turned in circles and then lay down. It was time for a snooze!

When Gypsy woke up, she decided to stay. She spent the whole afternoon sitting in the sunny warmth of the trampoline.

11

The man who lived in the house discovered Gypsy on his trampoline. It was a funny sight. He left the gate open, hoping she would leave. He didn't want to go near her because he didn't want to scare her.

His dog was named Gypsy, too. When his Gypsy started to leave by the gate, he said, "Gypsy, you stay right here."

Zach's Gypsy heard the order from the man and stayed on the trampoline.

The man thought it was strange that she wouldn't leave.

Zach's school day came to an end. He was still thinking about getting home to his puppy. "God, the best thing in my life is my dog, Gypsy. I can hardly wait to get home to her."

After this really hard day at school, Zach walked fast and even ran a bit as he got closer to home. He couldn't wait to see Gypsy.

As he turned the corner into the driveway of his house, he saw the backyard gate open. He ran as fast as his legs would carry him and started calling, "Here, Gypsy. Here, Gypsy."

When Zach ran into the backyard, he didn't see Gypsy. He looked under the bushes and flowers, in corners, and in her dog house. She was gone. His heart pounded. He cried, "Gypsy. Gypsy."

He needed help, so he quickly called his mother at work.

"Mom," sobbed Zach, "Gypsy is gone and I don't know where to find her. What should I do?"

Mom said, "Zach, stop crying and listen to me. You must wipe the tears from your eyes so that you can find Gypsy. Whistle as you look for her so she will hear you. Look all over the neighborhood, under bushes, on porches, in trash cans, in regular places and strange places. See if she is playing with the neighbor dog. Ask all the children you meet if they have seen Gypsy. Call her so that she will run to you. When you find her, bring her home. Then, give her a cookie-bone and a hug."

Zach started looking for Gypsy. He tried whistling, but his whistle was weak. Gypsy would never hear him whistle. He looked high and low. There was no Gypsy.

He asked everyone he met, "Have you seen my dog? Her name is Gypsy." A lump in his throat made his voice squeak. He couldn't control it.

It took too long to walk all over the neighborhood. Zach needed a bike. He frowned when he remembered how he broke his red bike. He had left it in the driveway and his dad accidentally drove over it.

The next time he needed a bike, he took his dad's bike without even thinking. He started acting silly and ended up bumping into a curb. The bike wheel bent so that he couldn't ride it. He had to push it home.

His dad didn't say anything as he replaced the wheel. When he took it off the work bench, he said, "Zach, you can't ride my bike without asking my permission. You need to learn to be responsible."

Zach's face turned red as he said, "OK, Dad."

This was an emergency that could only be solved with the speed of Dad's sleek yellow bike. Even though Zach felt guilty, he decided to take the bike. Besides, Dad was out of town. He would be careful with Dad's bike and put it back into the garage in the exact same place.

Zach scurried back to his house. He checked the backyard once more but Gypsy had not returned. He opened the garage door. He saw his dad's bike. He memorized the position of the bike. When he came back home, he would put the bike back the way he found it. He was confident that Dad would never know.

He hopped on the bike, and rode it up and down the hill. His whistle returned. It was strong and loud. He whistled over and over so Gypsy would hear him.

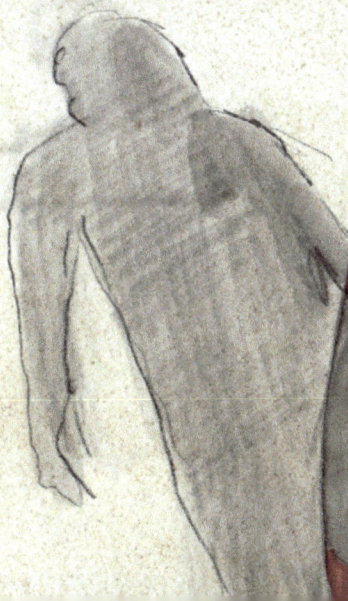

Zach called loudly, "Here, Gypsy. Here, Gypsy."

Zach pedaled faster and faster, and he rode further and further through the neighborhood. Still, no Gypsy.

As he rode, drops of rain began to pelt him. The rain became a gully-washer. It came down so hard that he could hardly see in front of him. Each drop of rain was stinging cold. He shivered.

Zach had to stop. As he tried to think, he leaned the bike against a tree. On the other side of the sidewalk was a beautiful house. The door opened. A pleasant lady with a big smile saw Zach standing in the rain with water dripping from his clothes and nose. She called to him to come into her house to get dry and to eat some delicious warm cookies.

Although, he was glad to get out of the rain, he knew that it was against his parent's rules. They didn't allow him to go into a stranger's house without them, but he thought it would be OK this one time. He told the nice lady about his missing Gypsy. She smiled and wished him luck.

As soon as the rain stopped, Zach bounded out of the door

to keep looking for Gypsy. He ran to the tree to get Dad's bike. It was gone. Oh, no! He scratched his head as he looked up and down the street. There was no bike. He was in so much trouble that he didn't know what to do.

He ran back to his home as fast as his legs would go. As he ran, he puffed and sobbed, thinking of the bad things that had happened. His head hurt and his stomach churned. What if Gypsy ran into the street and got hit by a car? What if someone stole her? What if she was lost and afraid? Was she hurt?

After a long run, he reached home. He scampered into the house. As the door slammed behind him, he dashed to the telephone to call his mom.

"Hello," she said.

He blubbered, "Gypsy is still lost." Then, he wailed, "I borrowed Dad's bike and it is gone, too!"

Mom exclaimed, "Zach, you stay home! I am coming."

Zach's little sister, Lisa, came home from school. When she learned that Gypsy was lost, she started crying with Zach. Lisa normally made it her business to annoy Zach. But, not today.

When Mom walked through the door, Zach and Lisa stopped crying. It was like the air whooshed out of a balloon. They felt relieved that Mom was there. She fixed things—kissed hurts and made life good.

But then, Zach's stomach flip-flopped. What if she couldn't fix things this time? His heart broke with a pain he had never felt before.

She said in a reassuring voice, "Calm down. We will find Gypsy."

Mom called the Animal Control Center. She explained, "Our dog, Gypsy, is missing. She is a beautiful, 3-month-old black Lab with a sparkle in her eye and a big grin."

Although, the ranger at the animal shelter was kind, he didn't think there was any hope. He said, "Lady, I am sorry. You will never find your Gypsy. She is gone. People who find pretty black Labs keep them. They will keep your fine Gypsy."

Mom said, "Please keep your eyes open for her. We love her very much and want her to come home."

Mom did not tell Zach and Lisa what the man told her. She put on a brave face, but her heart was aching, too! The Animal Control ranger knew about this sort of thing. However, Mom was convinced that he was wrong.

She made a plan. Photos of Gypsy sat on the mantle of the fireplace. Mom chose one for each of them to carry. They were going to look for their lost friend. Before they started, Mom told Zach and Lisa, "God will help us."

So they prayed: "God, you know where Gypsy is. Please keep her safe and help us bring her home. In Jesus' name. Amen."

They divided the neighborhood between the three of them. Zach looked over fences into backyards. He looked under bushes and places that were good for hiding. He showed Gypsy's photo to everyone he met. They all agreed Gypsy was a beautiful black dog. However, they had not seen her anywhere. He continued knocking on doors and pleading for help. No one knew where Gypsy might be. Zach wanted to quit looking and to go home to cry. But, he thought, "Just one more house—just one more try."

Lisa took the park behind the school where many families were watching the children practice soccer. She checked behind all the play equipment and around the flowers. She showed Gypsy's photo to everyone she saw. When they couldn't give her any information, Lisa thanked them for listening. She wiped the tear from her eye, then asked God, "Please, help me." All at once, Lisa smiled. She began running to find her family.

Mom knocked at every door on four blocks. She showed Gypsy's photo and asked, "Have you seen our Gypsy?"

They replied, "No."

Over and over in her head, she heard the man say, "Lady, you will never find your Gypsy." Mom prayed as she walked between the houses. She checked bushes, whistled and called to Gypsy. There was no answer. No one had seen the dog. Mom's heart was heavy. She felt discouraged.

Dusk came and soon it would be dark. The search would need to end soon.

She watched one more door close. As she stepped off the porch, she saw Lisa skipping toward her.

Mom thought, "Gypsy has been found." She hurried to Lisa.

Lisa bounced up and down as she said, "Mom, I have been praying for Gypsy. I know we will find her, and I want to be with you and Zach when it happens."

Mom felt a cold tinge of doubt and sadness surround her shoulders. She couldn't bear to think that Gypsy might not come home. She prayed, "Dear God, I know You answer prayers and, sometimes, You say 'No.' Today, will You please say 'Yes'? Please, God, lead us to Gypsy."

Mom took a deep breath and said, "Well, little Lisa, let's go look for Zach to see if he has found Gypsy."

They started up the hill. Lisa skipped on ahead, a beaming smile on her face. Mom walked slowly behind her. Her arms hung at her side and she kept her head down.

Just as they reached the top of the hill, Zach came around the corner. His grin stretched across his face. In his arms, he carried his big puppy.

Everyone laughed as they formed a noisy, jubilant parade bringing Gypsy home. As soon as they got inside the house, they gathered on the den floor around Gypsy to welcome her home. Then, Zach told his story:

Zach's legs felt like lead. He could hardly pick them up to walk any further. He wanted to turn around and go home. But, he decided to go to one last house.

He knocked on the door. When a man opened the door, Zach showed him Gypsy's picture and asked, "Have you seen my dog, Gypsy? She's lost."

The man chuckled and said, "I know exactly where your Gypsy is."

The man motioned for Zach to follow him and led him to the backyard.

There was Gypsy, bouncing on the trampoline and wiggling her whole body as she jumped down. She ran to Zach.

Zach scooped her up. He laughed so hard that he dropped to the ground. He rolled around with Gypsy. She licked his face all over.

The man started laughing. "My dog is named Gypsy, too. Your Gypsy is very happy to see you."

Zach said to his mom, "The lost is found."

The happy family roared with laughter. God had answered Zach's prayer even before Zach had prayed for Gypsy's safety.

Then, Mom said to Zach, "All that was lost has not been found. You still need to find Dad's bike."

Zach had already forgotten about it. He rolled his eyes and said, "M-U-T-H-E-R. We'll never find it."

Mom thought about it a moment. "God helped us find Gypsy when we thought it would be impossible. Why wouldn't He help us find Dad's bike? Do you remember what it says in James 4:2? It says, 'You do not have because you do not ask God.' I think we should ask God to help us find everything that is lost."

The family prayed together: "Dear God, thank You for helping find Gypsy. Our hearts are so happy. Please go with us to find the lost bicycle so that we can put it in the garage for Dad.

"In Jesus' name. AMEN."

Then, the family marched to the car. Mom led the way. Lisa followed. Zach dragged his feet behind them. He sat in the front seat so he could guide Mom to the tree where he placed Dad's bike. They drove up and down the hill, around a curve, and made two more turns. It was a long trip from Zach's house to the tree.

Finally Zach announced, "Stop. This is the place."

Mom parked the car in front of the big tree, but Dad's bike wasn't there. They looked from tree to tree but they didn't see Dad's bike. They scanned the porches and driveways up and down the street.

All at once, they noticed that the garage door for the next house was closing. Before it was completely down, they saw Dad's yellow bike inside.

"Oh!" they said in unison. Then, they all pointed at the closed garage door.

They looked at each other, their eyes wide. How could this be? How could they find the bike so easily?

Zach asked, "How will you get the bike?"

Mom winked and said, "Watch."

She marched up to the house and rang the doorbell. A pretty woman in a business suit came to the door.

Mom said, "I have come for our bike which is in your garage."

The lady smiled a broad smile. She said, "I just came home from work. I noticed the yellow bike and wondered why it was in my garage."

She turned to her children to ask, "Why is the yellow bike in our garage?"

Her son said, "We rescued the bike from the rain."

His sister added, "Rain is very bad for a beautiful yellow bike."

Mom thanked everyone for taking good care of the bike.

God's timing was exactly perfect. If Mom, Zach and Lisa had arrived one minute later, the garage door would have been closed. They would not have seen the bicycle.

Lisa and Zach picked the bicycle up and twisted it just right to make it fit into the back of the car. Then, they all piled into the car to take Dad's beautiful yellow bike home.

Before Mom turned the key to start the car, Zach became quiet. "Mom, something else got lost today."

Mom rolled her eyes in disbelief. "How could there be more?"

Zach continued, "It was me. I felt lost because I was having a hard time in school. Today, God showed me that He cares about me and will help me with things too big for me. I learned there are many things impossible for me, but not for God. He protected Gypsy and helped when I made a bad choice to disobey Dad. I gave up because I thought it was all impossible, but God simply opened a garage door to show me there is no door He cannot open, no problem that He cannot solve. Nothing is beyond His control. God used these lost things to show me that He has His eye on me. I am not lost."

Soon, they arrived home and Mom parked the car in the driveway. Zach pulled the yellow bike out of the car and placed it exactly where it belonged. Even Gypsy was happy to see the bike back in its right place. She wagged her tail and woofed.

Zach laughed, "This has been a great day. Yep, the best day of my life."

Yes, everyone was happy because they learned that God answers prayer and finds everything that is lost.

GOOD NEWS: God loves you and knows all about you. He even knows how many hairs are on your head. He loves and pursues you.

Luke 19:10
"For the Son of Man came to seek and to save the lost."

John 3:16-18
"For God so loved the world that he gave his one and only Son, that whoever believes in him shall not perish but have eternal life. For God did not send his Son into the world to condemn the world, but to save the world through him. Whoever believes in him is not condemned, but whoever does not believe stands condemned already because they have not believed in the name of God's one and only Son."

Romans 3:23-24
...for all have sinned and fall short of the glory of God, and all are justified freely by his grace through the redemption that came by Christ Jesus.

Ephesians 2:8-9
For it is by grace you have been saved, through faith—and this is not from yourselves, it is the gift of God—not by works, so that no one can boast.

Romans 5:8
But God demonstrates his own love for us in this: While we were still sinners, Christ died for us.

Romans 10:9
If you declare with your mouth, "Jesus is Lord," and believe in your heart that God raised him from the dead, you will be saved.

BIBLE
New International Version